Key Stage 2

Vocabulary

Carol Matchett

Name *Ben Cook*

Schofield&Sims

Introduction

The English language is amazing – there are so many words to choose from. The more words you know, the easier it is for you to read and write well.

This book will help you to develop your 'word power' by encouraging you to take an interest in words. It shows you how to understand words and how to choose the best words when writing. The examples will help you to see why words are important, and the activities will give you practice in using them.

Finding your way around this book

Before you start using this book, write your name in the name box on the first page. Then decide how to begin. If you want a complete course on improving your vocabulary, you should work right through the book from beginning to end.

Another way to use the book is to dip into it when you want to find out about a particular topic. The contents page will help you to find the pages you need. Whichever way you choose, don't try to do too much at once – it's better to work through the book in short bursts.

When you have found the topic you want to study, look out for these icons, which mark different parts of the text.

 **Activities**

This icon shows you the activities that you should complete. You write your answers in the spaces provided. After you have worked through all the activities on the page, turn to pages 33 to 40 to check your answers. When you are sure that you understand the topic, put a tick in the box beside it on the Contents page. On page 32 you will find suggestions for some projects (**Now you try!**), which will give you even more opportunities to improve your vocabulary.

 **Explanation**

This text explains the topic and gives examples. Read it before you start the activities.

Information

This text gives you background information about the history of words in the English Language. Surprise your friends with some fascinating facts!

 **Reference books**

These icons show that you will need a **dictionary** (D) or a **thesaurus** (T) when you are working through these pages.

Contents

Tick the box when you have worked through the topic.

Understanding words

Good readers and writers have 'word power'. They understand lots of words – and they know when and how to use them.

When you are reading or listening, you will often come across new words that you have not seen or heard before. You could just ignore them. But that won't help you to improve your word power. Instead, try asking yourself what the word means. Once you know what a word means, it will be stored in your word memory so that you can use it in the future.

1. Here are some words that you might come across when reading. Do you know what they mean? Write down the meaning of as many of the words as you can.

Don't worry if you don't know the meaning of all of the words. That's what this book is all about – learning new words.

	Word	Meaning
a)	scowl	
b)	vain	
c)	billow	
d)	plunge	
e)	trembling	
f)	commence	
g)	location	
h)	isolated	
i)	adequate	

Did you know... There are probably more than a million words in the English language – but no-one knows for sure. The words are impossible to count, because more and more new ones are always being invented.

The meaning of words

Quite often you can work out what a word means from the way it is **used** in a sentence.

For example: This train **terminates** at the next station. Will all passengers please get ready to leave the train.

From reading the rest of the sentence, you can guess that the word *terminates* means *'stops'* or *'comes to an end'*.

1. Read these sentences and try to work out the **meaning** of the word that is underlined. Look at the words in the box, and circle the word that gives the closest meaning.

a) The house made out of bricks was good and <u>sturdy</u>.

plain	weak
small	strong

b) We gasped when we saw the table, piled with <u>delectable</u> food.

smelly	horrid
cold	tasty

c) The team was <u>eliminated from</u> the competition when it lost in the third round.

knocked out of	added to
moved from	started in

d) The sails on the windmill began to <u>rotate</u>.

fall off	fly away
stand still	go round

e) Luckily the police were able to <u>thwart</u> the robber's getaway.

help	miss
whack	stop

f) It was not the *real* FA Cup – it was just a <u>replica</u>.

picture	copy
person	surprise

g) The ice on the roads made them <u>treacherous</u>.

uneven	safe
dangerous	expensive

Think about how a word is used to get an idea of its meaning. Then use a **dictionary** to check whether your idea is right. A dictionary gives you **definitions** of words. For example, if you were to look up the word *definition* you might find:

definition *n.* stating the meaning of a word

The words in a dictionary are in **alphabetical order** to make it easy for you to find them.

1. To use a dictionary well you have to be able to scan quickly through the lists of words. Scan through a dictionary to find words to complete these lists.

a)

Six animals beginning with the letter 'b'
•
•
•
•
•
•

b)

Six trees beginning with the letter 'p'
•
•
•
•
•
•

2. Use a **dictionary** to check the **meaning** of three words from the activity on page 4. Write the **words** and the **definitions** in the boxes below.

Word	Dictionary definition

Word roots and derivations

Another way of understanding what words mean is to learn about how they are formed. Many words are formed by taking one word (a **root word**) and adding groups of letters called prefixes and suffixes to the beginning or end.

For example: act   act**ion**   act**ive**   act**ivity**   **in**active   **pro**active

All these words are formed from the root word *act*, so the meanings of these words are also linked.

1. Look closely at these words. Draw a circle round the **root word** and underline the **prefixes** and **suffixes** that have been added.

a) re(direct)ion

b) repossession

c) misinformation

d) enjoyment

e) imprisonment

f) disagreeable

g) unusually

h) returnable

i) deformed

Some **prefixes** change the meaning of the **root word** to make a word with the **opposite** meaning.

For example: active (meaning *'working'*)   **in**active (meaning *'**not** working'*).

It is important to learn these **prefixes**:

in	dis	de	un	non	im	il

2. Use prefixes from the list above to make the **opposite** form of each word.

a) ____ fuse

b) ____ easy

c) ____ polite

d) ____ code

e) ____ approve

f) ____ visible

g) ____ order

h) ____ sense

i) ____ patient

j) ____ certain

k) ____ legal

l) ____ human

m) ____ obey

n) ____ happy

o) ____ possible

Word roots and derivations

Some words are built from two familiar parts. **For example:**

telephoto

tele – as in *television*

photo – as in *photograph*

The *tele–* part of the word means *'far off'*. So the word *telephoto* refers to taking photographs of something that is far away. If you learn the meaning of word parts, you can work out the meaning of lots of words.

3. Here are some word parts and their meanings. Use a **dictionary** to find four words that start in the same way. The first one is done for you.

a)	**tele** meaning *'far off'*	telephone, telescope, telegraph, teleport
b)	**auto** meaning *'self'*	
c)	**super** meaning *'more than'*	
d)	**trans** meaning *'across'*	
e)	**micro** meaning *'small'*	

4. Form four whole words from these word parts.

mega   inter   aero

marine   plane   phone

sub   national

_____ _____

_____ _____

Did you know...? Many word roots come from Latin and Ancient Greek, and inventors often use them when they need to make up a word for something new. For example, telephones and televisions were invented in the twentieth century, but the word *tele* was used in Ancient Greece many hundreds of years earlier.

Homographs

 **Homographs** are words that **look the same** because they have the **same spelling**, but have **different meanings**.

For example:

bark → **1.** noise made by a dog

2. the woody outer layer of a tree trunk

Look at how these words are **used**. The rest of the sentence will help you to decide which meaning is correct.

1. Tick the correct meaning of the **homograph** in each sentence.

a) We sat on the grassy **bank** and watched the river.
1. a slope ☐
2. a place for keeping money ☐

b) The king **rose** to his feet as the crowds cheered.
1. a flower ☐
2. got up ☐

c) We recorded the information on a **table**.
1. facts shown in columns ☐
2. a piece of furniture ☐

2. Use a **dictionary** to help you find different meanings of these words.

a) fan
Meaning **1.** _____
Meaning **2.** _____

b) train
Meaning **1.** _____
Meaning **2.** _____
Meaning **3.** _____

Did you know...? Homographs exist because English developed over a long period. One version of a word would already exist and then another would be added. No-one noticed until centuries later – but by then everyone was already using both words! For example, *bark* meaning *'the noise made by a dog'* is an Old English word, while *bark* meaning *'the woody outer layer of a tree trunk'* was a Norse word, added later.

It is a good idea to collect interesting words that you meet when reading – particularly words that you could use in your writing. Make sure you understand exactly what a word means if you plan to use it yourself.

For example: If you know that the word *ecstatic* means '*thrilled*', you can use it to describe:

the fans when their team scores a goal...

the person who has just won the lottery...

your brother given tickets to see his favourite band...

1. Here are five interesting words. Write down the meaning of each, using a **dictionary** to help you.

a) | **morsel** | Definition: _____

b) | **illuminated** | Definition: _____

c) | **ramshackle** | Definition: _____

d) | **dismal** | Definition: _____

e) | **exquisite** | Definition: _____

2. Now decide which word fits in each of these sentences. Write the word in the space.

a) The house was a _____ , run-down sort of place.

b) There was not a _____ of food left in the house.

c) The carvings on the box were _____.

d) It was a _____ day – it never stopped raining.

e) The trees were _____ by the soft moonlight.

Did you know... You have two lots of words in your word memory – the words that you *understand* and the words that you *use*. You will probably know and understand a lot more words than you use.

Choosing and using words

When you are writing, **don't use the first word that comes into your head**. You will come up with a more interesting or more accurate word if you think again.

For example: The man **walked** down the street.

Walked is a word that you use without thinking.

If you think, you will come up with lots of better words.

For example: strolled   marched   strode   plodded

1. Here are some sentences that use ordinary words, which come into your head straightaway. See if you can think of a **better word** to replace the word that has been crossed out.

a) There was a ~~big~~ _____ pile of rubbish by the door.

b) I enjoyed the book. It was very ~~good~~ _____.

c) We talked to the old lady for a while – she seemed very ~~nice~~ _____.

d) I ~~got~~ _____ a prize for winning the competition.

e) I was ~~scared~~ _____ by the sudden noise.

f) The boy looked very ~~sad~~ _____ .

2. Write down as many doing words as you can to describe how a person might move across the room. Two examples have already been written in the box.

creep   jump

Brainstorming words

Before you start writing about a subject, think of all the words you **could** use. Then look at them and pick the most suitable ones. Brainstorming or thought-mapping can help you to do this. This is what you do.

1. Write the name of the subject in the middle of a piece of paper.

2. Round the outside, write words that the subject makes you think of.

3. Outside those words, write more words to describe them.

... and so on, until your piece of paper is full!

1. Complete this brainstorm/thought map. See how many words you can think of to describe the sea.

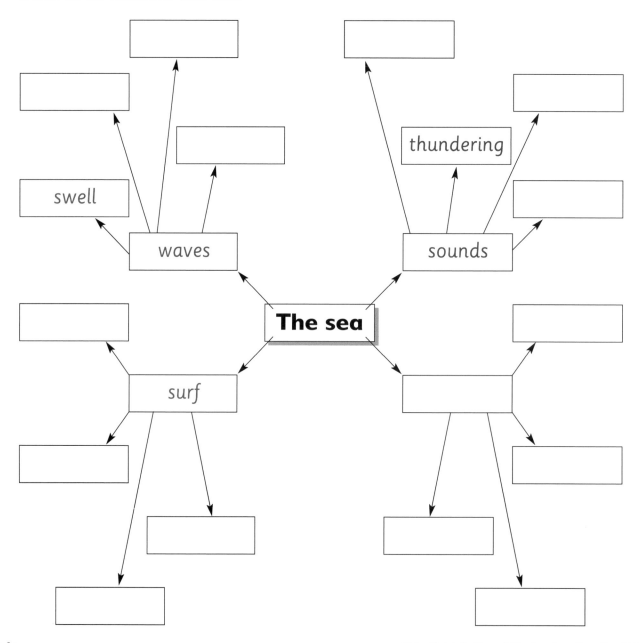

Synonyms

Synonyms are words that **mean the same** or **nearly the same**. Many words have synonyms, and this is useful. You don't need to use the same word again and again – instead, you can use a synonym.

For example: He walked along the **dark** path until he came to the **dark** building. The sky above was **dark**.

It sounds much better if you write:

He walked along the **shadowy** path until he came to the **unlit** building. The sky above was **gloomy**.

Shadowy, unlit and *gloomy* are synonyms for *dark*.

1. Match up pairs of words that have the **same or similar meanings**. Write the pairs of **synonyms** in the column on the right.

amusing	adore	_amusing_	and	_humorous_
angry	penniless		and	
strong	intelligent		and	
stop	humorous		and	
clever	assist		and	
like	prevent		and	
poor	powerful		and	
help	annoyed		and	

2. Write down a **synonym** for each of these words.

a) great _____

b) horrible _____

c) rich _____

d) little _____

e) stupid _____

f) quiet _____

Did you know... English has lots of words that mean nearly the same thing because it is a mixture of many languages. Some words used today existed in Old English, others were added by the Vikings – and more by the Normans when they invaded in 1066. Some of the words added by the Normans meant the same as words that already existed. All the words became part of the language and are still used today.

 We all need help sometimes in finding just the **right word**. That's why every writer should have a **thesaurus**. A thesaurus is a book that gives you a choice of words with a **similar meaning**.

For example: a **flash** of light

If you look up the word *flash* in a thesaurus you will find lots of words to choose from:

flash: beam ray spark blaze glare gleam glint flicker twinkle sparkle glitter shimmer

 1. Use a **thesaurus** to find lots of words with the **same or similar meanings** to these words.

a) **beautiful**

b) **happy**

c) **bright**

d) **very**

e) **throw**

Did you know...? Peter Mark Roget wrote a thesaurus in 1852. He said that the book was designed to help with 'the expression of ideas and assist in Literary Composition'. The word *thesaurus* comes from an Ancient Greek word meaning *'a treasury or store'* – and that's what a thesaurus is: a store of useful words.

Choosing the exact word

Not all the words given in a thesaurus mean exactly the same as the word you looked up. They may have **similar** meanings, but not **exactly** the same. When you use a thesaurus, you still have to decide which word describes exactly what you are trying to say.

For example: Was the **flash** of light...

a **beam** of light?   a **spark** of light?   a **glare** of light?   or a **flicker** of light?

1. Here are some words that you might use instead of the word *sad*. Choose the **best word** to use in each sentence.

sad:	unhappy	tearful	miserable	downhearted

a) The girl sobbed and looked up at me with a _____ face.

b) Ashia had a cold and was feeling _____ .

c) When we let in the fifth goal we were quite _____.

d) We were _____ about the decision but could do nothing.

2. Here are some words that you might use instead of the word *said*. Choose the **best word** to use in each sentence.

said:	yelled	asked	pleaded	laughed	whispered

a) 'Shh, or they will hear you,' _____ Lee.

b) 'Where do you live?' _____ Michael.

c) 'Help! Let me out of here!' _____ Charlotte.

d) 'You must be joking!' _____ Sheenia.

e) 'It's my turn. Let me try,' _____ Ravi.

Shades of meaning

Words that you find in a thesaurus will have different 'shades of meaning'.

For example:

angry: irritated annoyed displeased cross livid enraged furious

suggests a mild anger

suggests much stronger feelings

It is important to choose the word that has exactly the **right meaning** for your writing.

1. Sort these words into two sets to show their **different shades of meaning**.

a) It was a **hot** day.

hot:

| warm scorching boiling sweltering mild fine |

Fairly hot	**Very hot**

b) I was **happy** to be there.

happy:

| glad delighted thrilled pleased joyful content |

Fairly happy	**Very happy**

c) We **walked** to school.

walked:

| strode plodded trudged sauntered marched strolled |

Fairly slowly	**Fairly quickly**

Being precise

When choosing words, be as **precise** as possible. If you are writing about a shop, the word *shop* is **vague**. Instead you need a word that describes the shop **exactly**.

For example:

shop: supermarket, department store, baker, sweetshop, butcher, delicatessen, health-food shop, bookshop, newsagents, shoe shop, toyshop, florist

▲

One of these words would be a better choice, because each describes a **particular type** of shop.

1. Find words that could be used in place of these vague words.

a)

book
dictionary

b)

flower
rose

c)

house
bungalow

2. Improve these sentences by changing the word in bold print to **a more precise** one.

a) I watched the **insect** _____ land on the leaf.

b) The **bird** _____ sang beautifully in the tree outside the window.

c) I put the **book** _____ in my bag.

d) We planted some **flowers** _____ in the garden.

e) Ranjit went to the **shop** _____ to spend his money.

f) The Prince picked the golden **fruit** _____ from the tree.

Opposites or antonyms

If you look in a thesaurus, you may find that the **opposites** or **antonyms** of words are given.

For example: **young**–old   **hot**–cold   **start**–stop   **boy**–girl
happy–unhappy

Some words have more than one antonym.

For example: **silly** (*antonyms*): wise   sensible   clever   intelligent.

I. Match the **opposites** or **antonyms**. Write the pairs of words on the right.

easy	negative
ancient	rough
smooth	cowardly
close	difficult
positive	distant
huge	modern
cheerful	tiny
heroic	glum

_____easy_____ and _____difficult_____

_____ and _____

_____ and _____

_____ and _____

_____ and _____

_____ and _____

_____ and _____

_____ and _____

2. Complete these sentences using pairs of **antonyms**.

a) Cinderella's sisters were _____ but the Fairy Godmother was

_____ .

b) The Giant was _____ but Jack was _____ .

c) The hare was _____ but the tortoise was _____ .

d) Harry Potter is _____ but Voldemort is _____ .

e) Robin Hood was _____ but the Sheriff of Nottingham was

_____ .

The right words for the situation

When looking for the right word, think about the people who will read your writing. Words you use when talking to people you know well might sound out of place when you are writing to someone you do not know or want to impress.

For example: Lots of love   See ya!   CU...   Yours faithfully   Yours sincerely

These are all ways of ending a letter.

You could use the first three of these when writing to a friend, but only the last two would be suitable for a formal letter.

1. Here are some different ways of saying the same thing. Decide which you would use if writing **to a friend** and which you would use **to impress**. Complete the labels.

a) The special offer was **a rip-off**. ▶   to a friend

The special offer was **misleading**. ▶   to impress

b) They **blew** the money. ▶

They **squandered** the money. ▶

c) His haircut was **very fashionable**. ▶

His haircut was **real cool**. ▶

d) Jon felt **woozy**. ▶

Jon felt **light-headed**. ▶

e) I am **quite dehydrated**. ▶

I am **gasping for a drink**. ▶

f) He was a rather **dubious** character. ▶

He was a rather **shady** character. ▶

If you are writing something formal, use formal words. Think about what sort of words the person you are writing to might use and use similar language yourself. You can look words up in a **thesaurus** to help you find more **formal** versions.

For example, if you want a more formal word for *cheeky* you have these words to choose from: **cheeky**: impertinent   insolent   disrespectful   forward

1. Use a **thesaurus** to help you find more **formal** words to use in place of these words. The first one has been done for you.

a) **cheap:** | *inexpensive, reasonable, economical, affordable*

b) **give:**

c) **silly:**

d) **ugly:**

e) **smell:**

f) **easy:**

g) **test:**

h) **ask:**

Did you know... There has always been formal language and everyday language. After the Normans invaded Britain in 1066, all the most powerful people in the country spoke French. Lots of official words that we still use today were added at this time and they came originally from French: for example, *accuse*, *pardon*, *request*, *purchase*. Other official-sounding words came from Latin, which was the language used by the Church: for example, *formal*, *include*, *respect*.

Our changing language – new words

New words are always being added to the language. If there is a new idea or invention, a **new word** is needed to describe it. This century, the development of the internet has added many new words.

For example: internet   intranet   hyperlink   webcam   download

These words are made up of words, or bits of words, that **already existed**.
Lots of new words are made in this way.

1. Look closely at these words. Write down the two words that have been blended together to form a **new word**. (Use a dictionary to help you.)

a) Chunnel = | channel | + | tunnel |

b) heliport = | | + | |

c) smog = | | + | |

d) brunch = | | + | |

e) motel = | | + | |

2. Many **new words** are **old words** with a **new meaning**. Write in the **new meaning** for each of these words.

a) web

Original meaning: _a woven fabric or a spider's cobweb_

New meaning: _____

_____

b) text

Original meaning: _printed words_

New meaning: _____

_____

Old words

Some words fall out of use over time – they become old-fashioned, so people use them less and less and eventually stop using them at all.

For example:

sooth   anon

It is important to know about old words like these because you might find them in books written a long time ago.

---

1. Sort these words into **older words** that are not used much today and **newer words** that are used often.

	Older words	**Newer words**
neckerchief farthing Velcro superstar quoth flagon clarion computer rocket trainers video parlour		

2. Some words die out because the item they describe has been replaced by a newer invention. Write the names of the modern versions of these items, and draw a picture of each.

a)

quill _____

c)

carriage _____

b)
gramophone _____

d)
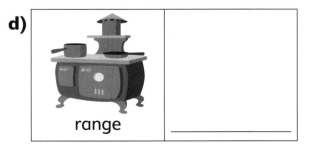
range _____

Words borrowed from other languages

Some words in the English language have been 'borrowed' from other languages. This explains some strange spellings.

For example:

banana	guitar	tobacco	Spanish
shampoo	cheetah	bangle	Hindi
judo	tycoon	karaoke	Japanese

1. Look closely at the words below. Draw a circle round the words that you think came from **another language**. Both the **spelling** and the **meaning** will give you a clue.

hand	café	safari	small
ski	run	pyjamas	floor
house	dish	kiosk	bamboo
plant	anorak	cat	volcano

2. Choose the **language** that you think these food words came from, and write it in the box.

a) pasta

b) naan

c) sushi

d) balti

e) tortilla

f) tandoori

g) risotto

h) spaghetti

Urdu

Spanish

Japanese

Italian

Did you know...

English has always borrowed words from other languages. As explorers travelled to different countries, words were added from Europe, the Americas, India, Australia and New Zealand. For example, Elizabethan explorers travelled to the New World (America) and came back with words such as *chocolate*, *tomato* and *tobacco*.

Words derived from other words

Sometimes a new word is created from an old word with **prefixes** and **suffixes** added to it. For example, the word *elastic* first came into the English language in the seventeenth century. Then new words were formed from this root word:

elastic ▶ elastic**ated** elastic**ity**

A group of words like this is called a **'word family'**, because all the words are related to the **root word**.

1. Use a **dictionary** to find three words that belong to the same **word family** as the first word.

a) colour ▶ _____ _____ _____

b) magnet ▶ _____ _____ _____

c) art ▶ _____ _____ _____

d) care ▶ _____ _____ _____

e) happy ▶ _____ _____ _____

f) move ▶ _____ _____ _____

2. Add one of these **suffixes** to each **root word** to make another word. You can use a suffix more than once.

able	ic	en	al	ship	hood	ist

a) | poet | |

e) | member | |

i) | novel | |

b) | deaf | |

f) | drink | |

j) | person | |

c) | child | |

g) | balloon | |

k) | agree | |

d) | origin | |

h) | photograph | |

l) | less | |

Forming nouns, verbs and adjectives

Different **types** or **classes of words** are used in different ways. **Verbs** describe actions, **nouns** are naming words and **adjectives** are describing words. If you add a **suffix** to the end of a word, you change the way it is used.

For example:

sweet (an adjective)

sweet**en** (a verb)   sweet**ness** (noun)

1. Change these words into **adjectives** by adding a **suffix** from the box.

ful	able	less	y	ish	al

a) comfort_____   **e)** cheer_____   **i)** water_____

b) music_____   **f)** help_____   **j)** fool_____

c) fashion_____   **g)** harm_____   **k)** name_____

d) accident_____   **h)** child_____   **l)** snow_____

2. Change these words into **nouns** by selecting the correct **suffix** from the noun generator box. Write the nouns in the empty column – one has been done for you.

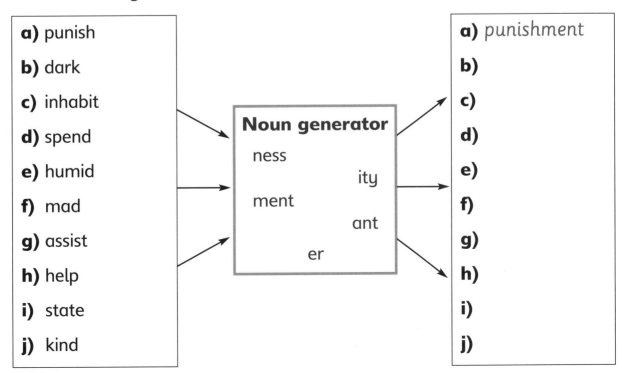

a) punish

b) dark

c) inhabit

d) spend

e) humid

f) mad

g) assist

h) help

i) state

j) kind

Noun generator

ness

ment

ity

ant

er

a) *punishment*

b)

c)

d)

e)

f)

g)

h)

i)

j)

Shortened words

Another way in which new words are formed is by **shortening a word** that already exists.

For example: mathematics ▶ maths   aeroplane ▶ plane

The meaning stays the same, and sometimes both the long **and** the short versions of the word will be used.

1. Complete these tables so that they show the **original** word and the **short** word that came from it.

	Original word	Shortened word
a)	omnibus	
b)	fanatic	
c)	stereophonic	
d)	vegetable	
e)	quadrangle	

	Original word	Shortened word
f)		demo
g)		fridge
h)		panto
i)		photo
j)		ad

2. Some words are shortened to the **initial** or **first letters**. Write down what the letters in these words stand for.

a) | **CD** | _____

b) | **ROM** | _____

c) | **WC** | _____

d) | **TV** | _____

Did you know... One of the most famous words made from initial letters is *OK* – but no-one is sure where this word comes from. It seems to have been used first in America in the 1830s and 1840s. It may be short for the humorous phrase *'oll korrect'*, or it may come from a slogan used by an American politician, Martin Van Buren, who had the nickname 'Old Kinderhook'.

Onomatopoeia

An onomatopoeic word **sounds like** the noise it describes.

For example: crash   pop   bleep   hum

It is easy to see, or hear, how these words were invented. Someone simply made up a word to describe a particular sound.

1. Sort these **onomatopoeic words** into three groups, according to the sort of sound they describe.

> bong   slosh   hum   splash   clatter   splish   crash   pitter-patter
> squeak   slop   swish   plop   boom   thud   swoosh

a) | **Watery sounds**

_____

_____

_____

_____

_____

b) | **Soft or quiet sounds**

_____

_____

_____

_____

_____

c) | **Loud sounds**

_____

_____

_____

_____

_____

2. Think of some **onomatopoeic words** to describe each of these sound pictures.

a) Someone falls into a duck pond.

b) You open a cupboard and everything falls out.

c) A car skids and crashes into a lamppost.

 **Did you know...** In the twentieth century, writers of comics and cartoon strips created lots of onomatopoeic words: for example, *bleep* and *zap*. Other examples go back hundreds of years. For example, the word *quack* was first used in the sixteenth century and *pop* goes back to the Middle Ages.

Inventing words

People often **invent new words** based on words that already exist. For example, the word *magazine* has been used since 1731, but in recent years people have taken the ending of this word and invented new words to add to it.

For example: **magazine** ▶ a thin book containing lots of different articles

fanzine ▶ a magazine for fans of a particular pop group

webzine ▶ a magazine that appears on the web

1. Use the clues to help you fill in the missing word.

a) _workaholic_ (Clue: Someone who can't stop working.)

b) _____ (Clue: Someone who can't stop shopping.)

c) _____ (Clue: Someone who can't stop eating chocolate.)

2. Make some more words with the same endings as these words. Use the words at the bottom to help you, or invent some words of your own.

a) water**proof** b) mar**athon** c) child-**friendly**

sound**proof**	walk**athon**	eco-friendly
proof	athon	-friendly
proof	athon	-friendly
proof	athon	-friendly

spell	**idiot**	**user**	**child**	**swim**
	burglar	**sleep**	**sing**	**teacher**
	family	**fire**	**euro**	

Origin of names

People, places and products have **names**. Names are special words that are used to set someone or something apart from all the others.

For example: Daljit Singh, Lucy Adams names of people

Portugal, Swansea, Charing Cross names of places

Coca-Cola, Elastoplast, Crunchie names of products

Originally, names were chosen because they **described** something about the person, place or product.

I. Here are some different types of English **surnames**. Add two more examples of each type.

a) Names that tell us what someone's job was

___Smith___ , ___Archer___ , _____ , _____

b) Names that tell us where someone lived

___Hill___ , ___Townsend___ , _____ , _____

c) Names ending with –son (meaning: 'son of')

___Robertson___ , ___Johnson___ , _____ , _____

2. Think of some towns and cities that have these clues about their past included in their name.

a) –ford (a place to cross a river)	b) –field (a field of open land)	c) –ton (a settlement or village)
Oxford	Wakefield	Bolton

Idioms

English is full of **idioms**. These are phrases that should **not be taken literally** because they do not mean exactly what they say.

For example: Ah, yes. George Brown. That name **rings a bell**!

The name doesn't really make a bell ring – it reminds us of something, or 'rings a bell' in our memory.

1. Here are some more **idioms**. Which saying is represented by each of the cartoons below?

Her face was a picture.   **I was thrilled to bits.**
We're all in the same boat.   **He's too big for his boots.**

a)

idiom: _____

_____

c)

idiom: _____

_____

b)

idiom: _____

_____

d)

idiom: _____

_____

2. Draw your own cartoons to represent these idioms.

a)

idiom: **Over the moon.**

b)

idiom: **In a jam.**

Did you know...

The idiom **'Put a sock in it'** means 'Be quiet'. It originates from the time when a gramophone player had no volume control. To make it quieter, you had to put a sock inside the trumpet.

The idiom **'Don't look a gift horse in the mouth'** means 'Don't be ungrateful when you are given something'. You can tell the age of a horse by looking at its teeth. If someone gives you a horse as a present and you immediately check its age in this way, you will seem very ungrateful.

The idiom **'It's raining cats and dogs'** means 'It is pouring with rain'. It may originate from a time when dogs and cats would sleep on the roof of a house. The roof got slippery when it rained and sometimes they would slide off!

Now you try!

Here are some reading and writing tasks that will help you to develop and use your growing vocabulary of words.

Treasury of words

Start collecting **interesting words**. Write them in a special notebook or on bits of paper that you can keep in a special box. Only collect words that you think you might find **useful** and make sure that you know what they **mean**.

Word of the day

Choose a word that you don't usually use and try to **use it** at least once during the day – either when speaking or writing. Make sure you know exactly what the word **means** so that you use it at the **right time** and in the **right way**.

Power read

Read something that you don't usually read, such as the news pages in the newspaper, part of a gardening book or a cookery magazine. This is a good way of finding new words that you have not met before. See if you can work out the **meaning** of these words. Use a **dictionary** to help you.

Call my Bluff

Play a game of 'Call my Bluff'. Choose an unusual word from the **dictionary** and write down the **definition**. Make up two false definitions. Give the three definitions to your friends and ask them to pick out the true one.

Name hunt

When you go out on a journey or go shopping, look out for the **names** of **places** (towns, streets, buildings, shops) and **products** (pop groups, cars, food and drink). See if you can work out why the names were chosen.

Comic sounds

Find some old comics that include comic strip stories. Look for examples of **onomatopoeic words** such as *THUMP! CLANK!* Try writing and drawing your own comic strip story, using as many onomatopoeic words as possible.

Answers

Page 4 **1.** *One meaning for each of the words is given below.*
a) scowl – an angry or menacing look
b) vain – proud or conceited about one's own appearance
c) billow – move in large waves or clouds
d) plunge – push or thrust something
e) trembling – shaking with fear or excitement
f) commence – begin or start
g) location – place
h) isolated – lonely
i) adequate – enough

Page 5 **1. a)** strong
b) tasty
c) knocked out of
d) go round
e) stop
f) copy
g) dangerous

Page 6 **1.** *Your lists may include the following, but there are many others.*

Six animals beginning with the letter 'b'	Six trees beginning with the letter 'p'
badger	pine
bat	plane
bear	pear
beaver	peach
bull	palm
buffalo	poplar

Page 7 **1.** *The root word is shown in* **bold** *– you should have drawn a circle round it.*
a) re**direct**ion
b) re**possess**ion
c) mis**inform**ation
d) en**joy**ment
e) im**prison**ment
f) dis**agree**able
g) un**usual**ly
h) re**turn**able
i) de**form**ed

2. a) defuse
b) uneasy
c) impolite
d) decode
e) disapprove
f) invisible
g) disorder
h) nonsense
i) impatient
j) uncertain
k) illegal
l) inhuman
m) disobey
n) unhappy
o) impossible

Page 8 **3.** *These are some of the words you might have found in the dictionary.*
a) tele – telephone, telescope, telegraph, teleport
b) auto – automatic, automate, automobile, autopilot
c) super – supernatural, supersonic, superstar, supermarket
d) trans – transplant, transport, transfer, transatlantic
e) micro – microscope, microcosm, microbe, microphone

Answers

4. *You will probably have formed the following words. If you have made any others, check them in the dictionary.*

megaphone   international   aeroplane   submarine

Page 9

1. **a)** 1. a slope
    b) 2. got up
    c) 1. facts shown in columns

2. **a)** fan → Meaning 1. a device for making cool air
           → Meaning 2. an enthusiastic supporter

    b) train → Meaning 1. a form of transport that runs on rails
            → Meaning 2. part of a dress that trails behind
            → Meaning 3. to practise something (particularly a sport) so as to get better at it

Page 10

1. **a)** morsel – a scrap or a very small piece
    b) illuminated – lit up
    c) ramshackle – rickety and tumbledown
    d) dismal – gloomy and dull
    e) exquisite – very fine or delicate

2. **a)** The house was a **ramshackle**, run-down sort of place.
    b) There was not a **morsel** of food left in the house.
    c) The carvings on the box were **exquisite**.
    d) It was a **dismal** day – it never stopped raining.
    e) The trees were **illuminated** by the soft moonlight.

Page 11

1. *These are just suggestions; you might have thought of some other interesting words to use.*
    a) There was **an enormous** pile of rubbish by the door.
    b) I enjoyed the book. It was very **interesting**.
    c) We talked to the old lady for a while – she seemed very **friendly**.
    d) I **received** a prize for winning the competition.
    e) I was **startled** by the sudden noise.
    f) The boy looked very **tearful**.

2. *These are some of the words that you might have chosen – there are lots more.*

creep	jump	hobble
hop	skip	dance
tiptoe	march	strut
trudge	waltz	shuffle
run	waddle	amble
dart	stride	tramp

Answers

Page 12 **1.** *These are just suggestions; you might have thought of some other words.*
waves: swell, ripples, breakers, wash
sounds: thundering, roaring, whooshing, whispering
surf: foaming, frothy, creamy, snowy
appearance: shimmering, grey-green, cloudy, glassy

Page 13 **1.** amusing and humorous
angry and annoyed
strong and powerful
stop and prevent
clever and intelligent
like and adore
poor and penniless
help and assist

2. *These are just suggestions, as these words have many synonyms.*
 a) great – wonderful
 b) horrible – awful
 c) rich – wealthy
 d) little – tiny
 e) stupid – foolish
 f) quiet – peaceful

Page 14 **1.** *These are just a few of the words you might have found in the thesaurus.*
 a) beautiful – attractive, lovely, gorgeous, stunning, enchanting
 b) happy – joyful, merry, pleased, delighted, content
 c) bright – gleaming, glistening, glowing, brilliant, dazzling
 d) very – extremely, terribly, absolutely, greatly, highly
 e) throw – hurl, sling, toss, fling, bowl

Page 15 **1.** *Here are some possible answers – yours may not be exactly the same.*
 a) The girl sobbed and looked up at me with a **tearful** face.
 b) Ashia had a cold and was feeling **miserable**.
 c) When we let in the fifth goal we were quite **downhearted**.
 d) We were **unhappy** about the decision but could do nothing.

2. **a)** 'Shh, or they will hear you,' **whispered** Lee.
 b) 'Where do you live?' **asked** Michael.
 c) 'Help! Let me out of here!' **yelled** Charlotte.
 d) 'You must be joking!' **laughed** Sheenia.
 e) 'It's my turn. Let me try,' **pleaded** Ravi.

Answers

Page 16

a) Fairly hot
warm, fine, mild

Very hot
scorching, boiling, sweltering

b) Fairly happy
glad, pleased, content

Very happy
delighted, thrilled, joyful

c) Fairly slowly
plodded, sauntered, strolled, trudged

Fairly quickly
strode, marched

Page 17

1. *These are just a few of the words you might have included in your lists.*

a) book	**b) flower**	**c) house**
dictionary	rose	bungalow
encyclopaedia	violet	manor house
atlas	daffodil	town house
guidebook	buttercup	cottage
storybook	primrose	mansion
telephone directory	tulip	farmhouse

2. *Here are a few possibilities – there are lots of other words you could have chosen.*

a) I watched the **butterfly** land on the leaf.

b) The **nightingale** sang beautifully in the tree outside the window.

c) I put the **photo album** in my bag.

d) We planted some **sunflowers** in the garden.

e) Ranjit went to the **toyshop** to spend his money.

f) The Prince picked the golden **pineapple** from the tree.

Page 18

1. easy and difficult
ancient and modern
smooth and rough
close and distant
positive and negative
huge and tiny
cheerful and glum
heroic and cowardly

2. *These are just suggestions – there are other pairs of antonyms that could be used.*

a) Cinderella's sisters were **cruel** but the Fairy Godmother was **kind**.

b) The Giant was **rich** but Jack was **penniless**.

c) The hare was **foolish** but the tortoise was **clever**.

d) Harry Potter is **good** but Voldemort is **evil**.

e) Robin Hood was **generous** but the Sheriff of Nottingham was **mean**.

Answers

1. **a)** a rip-off – to a friend
misleading – to impress
b) blew – to a friend
squandered – to impress
c) very fashionable – to impress
real cool – to a friend
d) woozy – to a friend
light-headed – to impress
e) quite dehydrated – to impress
gasping for a drink – to a friend
f) dubious – to impress
shady – to a friend

1. *These are just a few of the words that you might have found in the thesaurus.*
a) cheap – inexpensive, reasonable, economical, affordable
b) give – present, donate, award, provide
c) silly – irrational, absurd, idiotic, immature
d) ugly – unattractive, unsightly, hideous, offensive
e) smell – odour, fragrance, aroma, stench
f) easy – uncomplicated, effortless, straightforward, manageable
g) test – examine, assess, evaluate, investigate
h) ask – enquire, request, demand, appeal

1. *The new words have been formed as follows.*
a) Chunnel = channel + tunnel
b) heliport = helicopter + airport
c) smog = smoke + fog
d) brunch = breakfast + lunch
e) motel = motor + hotel

2. **a)** web – a network of information sources accessed by the internet
b) text – to send someone a message using a mobile phone

1.

Older words	New words
neckerchief	Velcro
farthing	superstar
quoth	computer
clarion	trainers
flagon	video
parlour	rocket

2. **a)** pen *or* biro   **c)** car *or* bus
b) CD-player *or* stereo   **d)** cooker

Answers

Page 23   **1.** *The words originally from another language are as follows.*
café   safari   ski   pyjamas   kiosk   bamboo   anorak   volcano

2.
a) pasta – Italian   **e)** tortilla – Spanish
b) naan – Urdu   **f)** tandoori – Urdu
c) sushi – Japanese   **g)** risotto – Italian
d) balti – Urdu   **h)** spaghetti – Italian

Page 24   **1.** *These are just some suggestions. You may have found other words from the same families.*
a) colour   ▶   colourful, colouring, colourless
b) magnet   ▶   magnetic, magnetise, magnetism
c) art   ▶   artist, artistic, artefact
d) care   ▶   careful, careless, caretaker
e) happy   ▶   happily, happiness, unhappy
f) move   ▶   movement, moveable, remover

2. *The new words should be as follows.*
a) poetic   **e)** membership   **i)** novelist
b) deafen   **f)** drinkable   **j)** personal
c) childhood   **g)** balloonist   **k)** agreeable
d) original   **h)** photographic **l)** lessen

Page 25   **1.** *In some cases you can make more than one word from the suffixes given – all of the following are correct. If you have made another word, check it in the dictionary.*
a) comfortable/comfortless   **e)** cheerful/cheery/cheerless   **i)** watery
b) musical   **f)** helpless/helpful   **j)** foolish
c) fashionable   **g)** harmful/harmless   **k)** nameless
d) accidental   **h)** childish/childless   **l)** snowy

2.
a) punishment   **f)** madness
b) darkness   **g)** assistant
c) inhabitant   **h)** helper
d) spender   **i)** statement
e) humidity   **j)** kindness

Answers

Page 26 **1.**

	Original word	Shortened word
a)	omnibus	**bus**
b)	fanatic	**fan**
c)	stereophonic	**stereo**
d)	vegetable	**veg**
e)	quadrangle	**quad**

	Original word	Shortened word
f)	**demonstration**	demo
g)	**refrigerator**	fridge
h)	**pantomime**	panto
i)	**photograph**	photo
j)	**advertisement**	ad

2.
- **a)** CD – compact disc
- **b)** ROM – read-only memory
- **c)** WC – water closet
- **d)** TV – television

Page 27 **1.**

a) **Watery sounds**	b) **Soft or quiet sounds**	c) **Loud sounds**
slosh	hum	bong
splash	squeak	clatter
splish	swoosh	crash
slop	swish	boom
plop	pitter-patter	thud

2. *These are just a few suggestions – you might have chosen other words.*
- **a)** Someone falls into a duck pond. – splash, plop, splat
- **b)** You open a cupboard and everything falls out. – clatter, crash, bang
- **c)** A car skids and crashes into a lamppost. – screech, clang, smash

Page 28 **1.**
- **a)** workaholic
- **b)** shopaholic
- **c)** chocaholic

2.

a)	b)	c)
waterproof	marathon	child-friendly
soundproof	walkathon	eco-friendly
burglarproof	swimathon	teacher-friendly
childproof	singathon	user-friendly
fireproof	sleepathon	euro-friendly
idiotproof	spellathon	family-friendly

Answers

Page 29   **1.**   *These are just a few of the many names you could have chosen.*
  a) Smith, Archer, Butcher, Baker
  b) Hill, Townsend, Woods, Rivers
  c) Robertson, Johnson, Jackson, Richardson

   2.   *These are just a few of the many place names you could have chosen.*

a) Oxford	**b)** Wakefield	**c)** Bolton
Bedford	Lichfield	Warrington
Bradford	Huddersfield	Buxton
Stratford	Sheffield	Preston
Salford	Mansfield	Brighton

Page 30   **1.**   *The following idioms are represented by the cartoons.*
  a) He's too big for his boots.
  b) I was thrilled to bits.
  c) Her face was a picture.
  d) We're all in the same boat.

Page 31   **2.**   *Your cartoons should show the following.*
  a) Someone looking very happy.
  b) Someone stuck somewhere, such as in a traffic jam.